The author and publishers would like to thank
Dr R. H. James MB, BS, FFARCS
for his help and advice
with the preparation of this book.

HAMISH HAMILTON CHILDREN'S BOOKS

Published by the Penguin Group
27 Wrights Lane, London W8 5TZ, England
Viking Penguin Inc., 40 West 23rd Street, New York, New York 10010, U.S.A.
Penguin Books Australia Ltd, Ringwood, Victoria, Australia
Penguin Books Canada Ltd, 2801 John Street, Markham, Ontario, Canada L3R 1B4
Penguin Books (N.Z.) Ltd, 182–190 Wairau Road, Auckland 10, New Zealand

Penguin Books Ltd, Registered Offices: Harmondsworth, Middlesex, England

First published in Great Britain 1984 by
Hamish Hamilton Children's Books

Reprinted 1985, 1987

British Library Cataloguing in Publication Data
Richardson, Joy
What happens when you sleep?
1. Sleep. – Juvenile literature
I. Title   II. Maclean, Colin, 1930–
III. Maclean, Moira
612'.821   QP425
ISBN 0 241 11226 5

Printed in Great Britain by
Cambus Litho, East Kilbride

What happens
when you
SLEEP?

Joy Richardson

Illustrated by
Colin and Moira Maclean

Hamish Hamilton · London

Time for bed
Sleepyhead!

Sleep is a mystery.
You go to sleep each night,
and before you know what
has happened . . .
it's morning again.

All day long your brain is busy.
Thousands of messages about things
you see and hear and feel
come into your brain.

The messages come into a special
collecting place in your brain.
Then they are sent on to the rest of
your brain for thinking about.

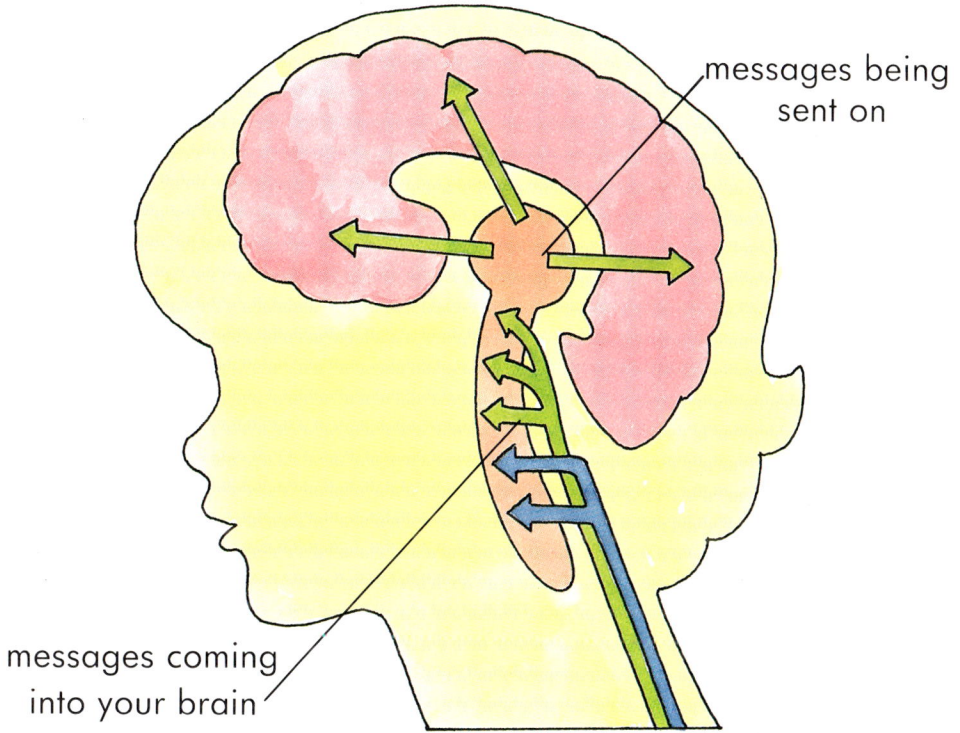

messages being
sent on

messages coming
into your brain

When it is time for sleep,
the messages stop being sent on.
This lets you fall asleep.

It can be difficult to get to sleep
if you are excited or
if you feel frightened.
Strong messages keep breaking out
of the collecting place in your brain.
They keep you awake.

Which of these things help you to feel ready for sleep?

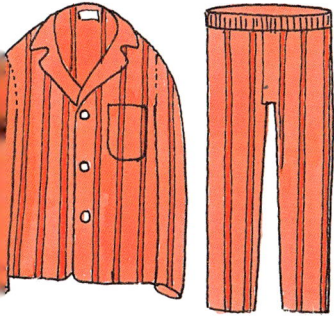
night clothes

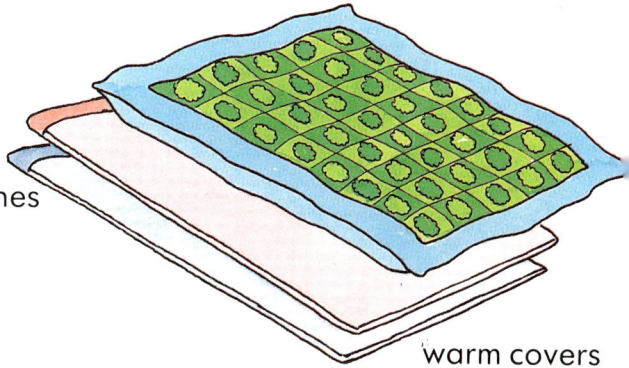
warm covers

a bedtime story

a cuddly toy

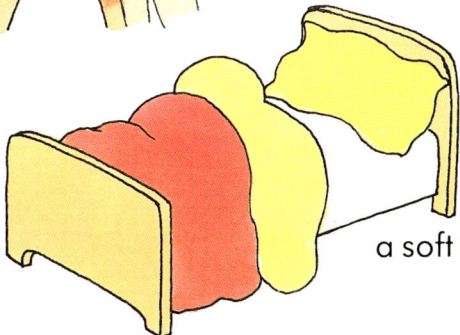
a soft bed

a dark room

Lie down on the floor,
as if you were getting ready for sleep.

Did you lie on your back
      or on your front
      or on your left side
      or on your right side?

Did you curl up small or
stretch out straight?

8

You do not lie the same way
all night long.
You toss and turn lots of times
in your sleep.
This stops you getting stiff
and sore.

When you get into bed
you shut your eyes.
Soon you feel drowsy.

Patterns and shapes
float in front of your eyes.
Sometimes you think strange thoughts.

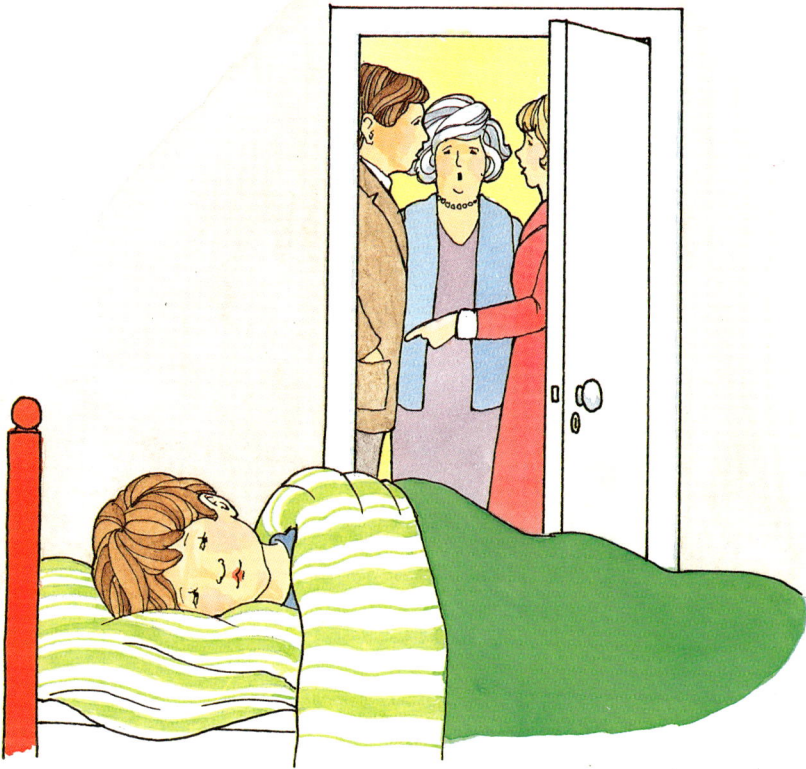

You fall asleep without knowing it.
At first you sleep lightly.
You might wake up if you heard
a noise.

Slowly you fall into deeper
and deeper sleep.

Lie down on the carpet.
Make your body stiff all over.
Ask a friend to lift your arm or
your leg off the ground and
let it go down again.

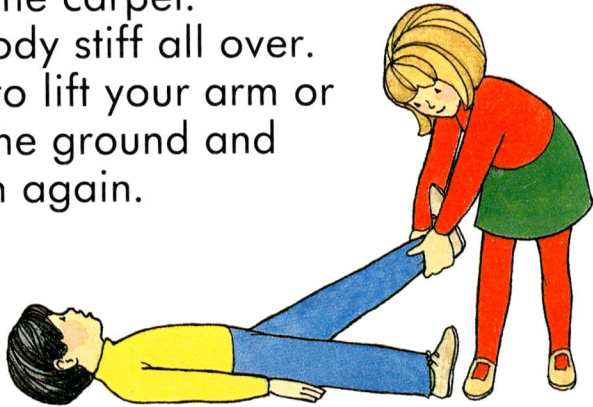

Now let your body relax so that
it is soft and floppy.
What happens now when your arm or
leg is lifted and dropped?

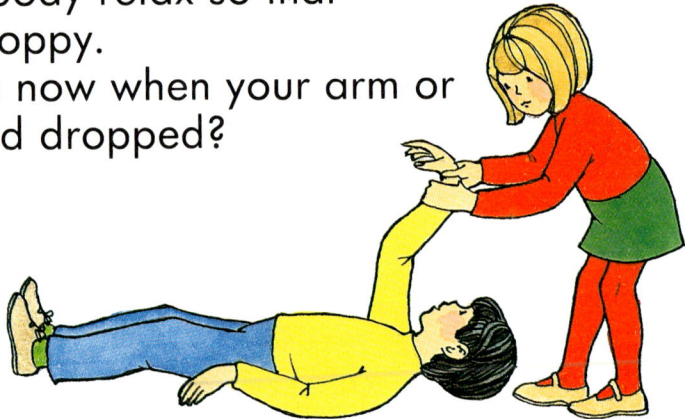

When you go to sleep your body
is relaxed like this.
Your muscles have a good rest.

Your heart and your lungs
go on working even when
you are asleep.

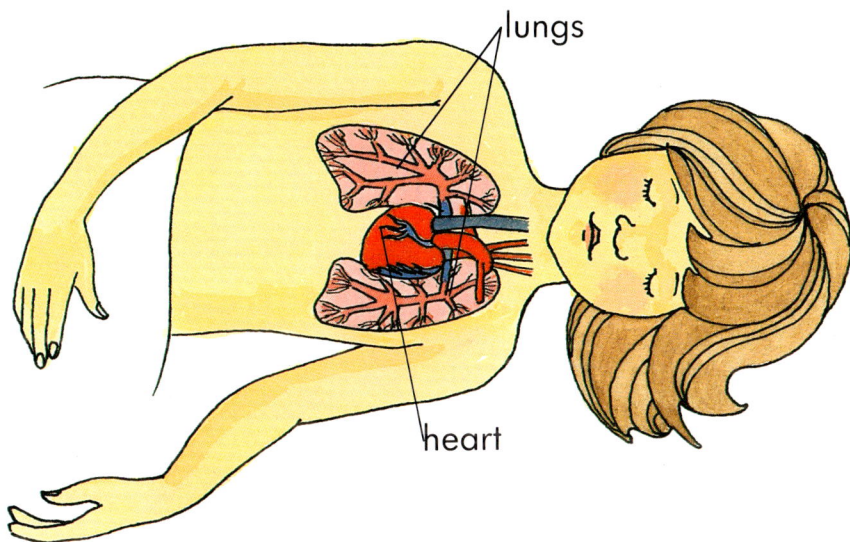

lungs

heart

But you use up less energy,
so you breathe more slowly and
your heart beats less often.

When you have fallen into a deep sleep,
something strange happens . . .
You begin to dream.

Dreaming is very important.
It is your brain's way of
sorting itself out.

You never know what you will
dream about.
Bits and pieces of things you have seen
and done and thought about
get jumbled up together.
They turn into a story.

These stories can be very odd.

When you dream,
your heart beats faster
and your eyes jerk about
under your eyelids.

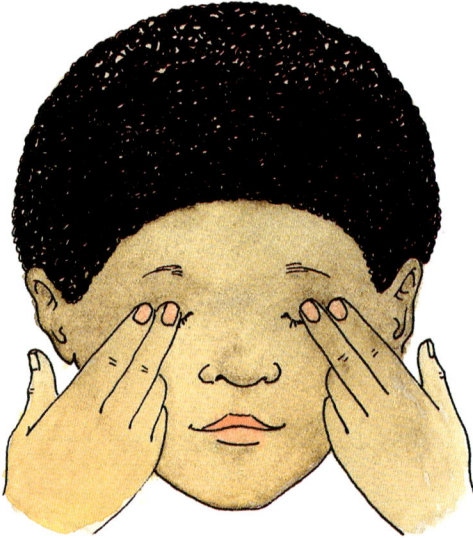

Close your eyes and put your
fingers gently on your eyelids.
Look up and down and
from side to side.
Can you feel your eyeballs moving?
They begin moving about like this
when you begin to dream.

16

Nightmares are nasty dreams.
You may cry or shout out in your sleep
because they seem so real.
They make you so frightened
that an urgent message is sent
to your brain to wake you up.

During the night you keep going
from light sleep,
to deep sleep,
to dreaming sleep.
You dream about five times a night.

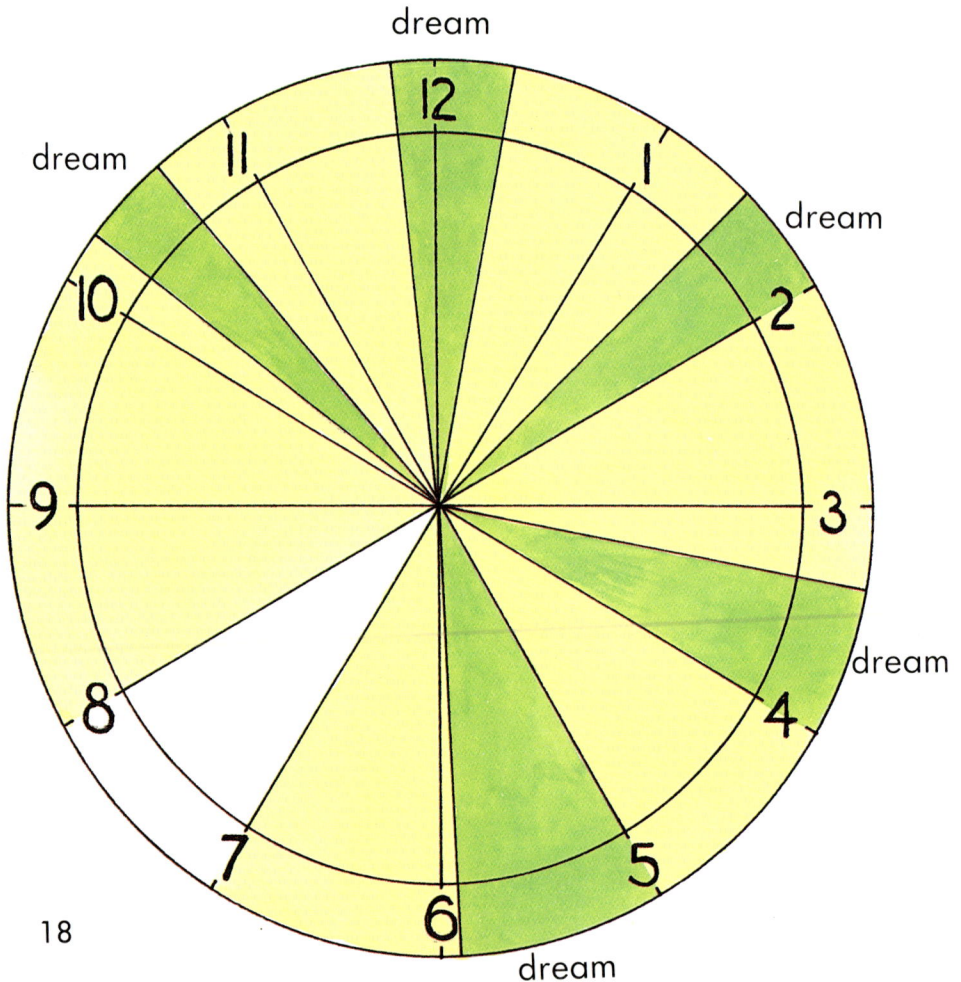

dream

dream

dream

dream

dream

12
1
2
3
4
5
6
7
8
9
10
11

18

You only remember a dream
if you wake up very soon afterwards.
If you go on sleeping,
the dream fades and vanishes away.

Everyone dreams at night,
but most dreams are forgotten.

Some people snore.

Put your head back and
let your mouth drop open.
Breathe in through your mouth.
Can you make a snoring sound?

People snore in their sleep while
their mouth muscles are relaxed.

If you need to go to the toilet
in the night, an urgent message
goes to your brain.
It wakes you up.

Children may wet the bed by mistake.
Their bodies are very relaxed and
the message has not yet learned
how to get through.

21

Your brain knows when it is time
to wake up in the morning.

If you are still asleep,
a loud noise or a bright light
will soon wake you.

You sleep with your eyes shut,
but your eyelids do not keep out
all the light.

Close your eyes and
turn towards the light.
What can you see?

Put your hands over your eyes.
What difference does that make?

You can tell if morning has come
even with your eyes shut.

Small babies sleep most of the time.
Children sleep 10 or 12 hours a night.
Grown-ups sleep about 8 hours a night.

Just think!
You have been asleep for
nearly half your life.
How many years is that?

INDEX